The Soul Garden

Words by Bethany Arrowsmith-Cooper

Illustrations by Grace Scott

Author: Bethany Arrowsmith-Cooper
Illustrations: Grace Scott, Graceful Designs

First Printing: 2019

ISBN 978-0-244-76555-2

Instagram: @soulgardenpoems
bethacpoetry@gmail.com
soulgarden.blog

Contents Page

The Empty Space Inside That Nobody Knows About

Here, again, I find myself
upon my tired bedroom floor, considering
the empty space inside that nobody knows about
and nothing more.

I wonder what will grow there
or if, indeed, it could be filled?
Whether one could plant a seed
and watch it   shoot

                    and blossom

                          and flourish

into the
most beautiful plant
your eyes have ever seen.

What if a small creature
no bigger than
the palm of your hand
were to scurry there
and burrow
and claim it as its own land?

What then?
At least
the empty space inside that nobody knows about
would be of some use.

It would have a purpose,
a place,
a reason to exist.

For now,
it is just an ache
that fails to fade away
with the kick of
strong morning coffee
and the half-hearted smiles
of strangers
as they make their way
to work
or the movies
or-   are they full themselves?

Or,
like me,
on my tired bedroom floor,
are they missing a component?

Like a mug   without its tea,

a cot   without its child,

a white canvas   without its artist.

If the space was filled   would it then be missed?

Perhaps, it is a garden.
With flowers
and bees
and butterflies!
Perhaps it is a space
one might,
someday, wish to hide
away from   (Because,
reality   sometimes.
and the rain clouds.   It rains.)

And, sometimes
the rain is so heavy that
the empty space inside that nobody knows about
cannot contain any more
and it floods
and the water spills out
and it is salty
and unpleasant
all over my
tired
bedroom
floor.

However,
I hope,
someday,
the empty space inside that nobody knows about
will be filled.

Until then
it remains empty-
-just a dull ache somewhere in my soul.

But, as the rain falls,
at least it will make
the flowers grow.

Shipwrecked

My lonely vessel lingers
Atop a vast expanse of deep brine.

No bird soars above me
Nor creature below,

Just the quiet waves,
This raft of mine,

And my heart,
A rhythm I have grown to know.

The sun welcomes my mornings,
with splendour and incandescent light.

In the evenings, an ocean of stars,
Dances over my head.

Nobody can hear me,
No shore is in sight,

I cry out to the wind,
And her whisper is my only friend.

I consider swimming ashore
whatever it entails.

Alas, it is much too far,
and I am much too weary.

The wind has been knocked
from my sails.

I consider drowning myself;

I lie awake,
listening to the curling waters below,

The gentle tumbling,
the sound of my breath.

I yearn for the deep
To send me to my home.

I may as well be sinking,
It would inconvenience me less.

On the Third Day

The night
spreads its shade
over the Earth.
Black,
and with it,
cold.

The twilight
casting shadows on
what once was beautiful:

Joy into sadness;
hope into fear;
light into dark.

The saviour,
the hero,
gone.

Panic rips across your face-

- would you abandon
me in this place?

- where are you
when I need you most?

The lights turn out
and, with them,
all hope

- a ghost.

But,
quietly comes the morning.

It isn't loud,
or roaring.
No triumphal entry
or grand arrival,
just lazy,
resting on the horizon
warming, again,
what once was black.

The shadowy fingers
retreat with day;
death's tombstone
is rolled away;

The sun is risen
once again
and floods with world
with light.

Quietly comes the morning,
the dawning,
the end to one more night.

35,000ft

At 35,000ft off the ground
you notice many things.
You see the tiny villages
and birds out on the wing.
The breathing, rippling ocean,
the life and soul of Home,
the veins that flow through field and plain
and valley far below.

The wrinkles of the Earth stand out
through vapour resting still,
and snow-kissed tops and crevices
and wisdom in each hill.
The clouds that once were dark and grey
now sit in glorious light,
and the endless blue surrounding
puts your worries out of sight.

At 35,000ft off the ground
your troubles seem so small,
for God so greatly loved the world
He graced us with His all

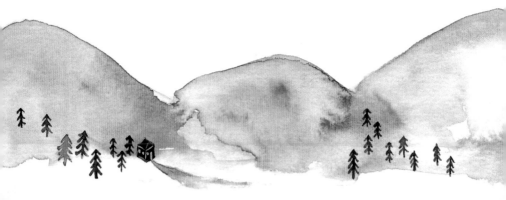

Did you not know?
Have you not heard?
The Lord is the
everlasting God
The Creator of the
ends of the earth
He will not grow
tired or weary
and his
understanding
no one can fathom

ISAIAH 40:28

One More Cup of Tea

Age did you no favours.
It bent your back
and brittled your bones
and broke your body down.
But, you were never defeated.
Your back, though it hurt, was helped
by that heated massager thing
you loved to use all the time;
the one that lit up and buzzed.
You let me try it, once,
that was enough.

Regardless of that,
your spirits were high
and there was always a slight
twinkle in your eye
when you told me stories
from "that time" long ago.
There's still so much I don't know.

You had a whole life
before we met,
adventures
and experiences
and moments,
now memories, intertwined.

You never did mind
if I arrived slightly late
because I always made your tea extra hot.
I knew you liked that a lot.

We didn't have much time together
but I know you'll be etched in my memory, forever,
so if I'll take one thing from our friendship,
it's this:
Even though you've watched
the world fall to bits
a countless number of times,
you always greeted me with a smile.

Then, you told me to
"behave myself"
with a chuckle,
and your smile grew.
The world didn't turn you bitter,
friend, your hope always shone through
like a candle in a very dark room.

And now, I know
that when I'm all grown up
and age is doing me no favours,
I want to be just like you.

- For Ian.

Change Your Lenses

When my mum takes off her glasses
she sees the world in a different way.
She slides them
over her nose
off her face
gives them a quick clean with the cloth
closes the arms tight
and snaps them shut
in her polka dot glasses case.

Then, she squints a little
because the world isn't all that clear.
The lines around the shapes
are blurred
unless they're right
under her nose.

When my mum takes off her glasses,
for a moment,
her perspective has changed.
But while everything
appears to be different,
everything is actually
just the same.

People Killed the Planet

A man sits, lonely, by the roadside
jangling his hat at passers-by,
but nobody sees him struggling there.
For the Beggar Man, there is no care.

What have we done to this gift of Home?
Compassion's at an all-time low.
The children cry, but no-one hears
because we're wrapped up
in our social world.

Pesticides killed all the bees,
we failed to keep the oceans clean,
the Barrier Reef's been bleached to death
- a crime resting on humanity's head -
Ice caps are melting,
sea levels rising,
animals fighting for survival
and yet you're still in denial
about Climate Change
and the impact we've had
on the world.

Governments are out of hand,
we let idiots near nuclear plans.
Breaking News!
It wasn't God who killed the world
but the consumerist regime.
The human condition of
me, myself and I,
where "want" turns into "need".

The luxuries of life have become
basic
human
rights.

While the Beggar Man
sits in the street
- his jangling hat
now by his feet -
curling into his jacket
because that's where
he'll spend the night.

Money makes the world go round
for those who can afford it,
but people live in poverty
and those with wealth ignore it.

Why give money for people's health
when you could spend it on yourself?!
Be filled temporarily by material gain
until the gaping hole comes back again.

Our selfishness and lack of love
have turned the lights out on the Earth.
The sun's gone down
but the stars won't shine
because there's no hope left above.

Year upon year the world will turn,
but the Human Race no more will stir
because people killed the planet.

A man sits, frozen, by the roadside;
in his icy death, he'll live,
and his jangling hat is silent
because there's no-one left to give.

Greater love has no one than this to lay down one's life for one's friends

JOHN 15:13

Bubblegum

Take my heart out of my chest
And fix it up with tape.
Put plasters over all the cracks
Before it is too late.
Stick bubblegum inside the holes
And cream on every bruise.
Can such a battered, patchwork heart
Ever be made new?

Take my heart out of my chest
(And all the pieces that are left)
Dig a hole in the dirt
And there my heart will plant.

How rare a thing it is,
To love,
But a painful one at that.

This Is a Love Poem

This is a love poem
but I'm not going to talk about romance.

It doesn't have
a fairy-tale ending
because true love almost never does.

Yes, love is patient
and love is kind,
but it's also
battered and
beaten and
bruised.

This kind of love isn't pretty.
It's unconditional,
non-judgemental,
counter-cultural
and true.

Love is
lying facedown in the mud with them
so they don't have to lie there alone.

Love is
joining them on the frontline of the battle
because they can't win the fight on their own.

Love is
holding their bloodied hand
after they've punched a hole in the wall
as big as the vacuum in their soul
and standing by them until their fears go.

Love never fails;
in the darkness
it is the light.

In the lost and broken-hearted
it is revival,
redemption,
rehabilitation.
We are a nation
bathed in hatred
but it's senseless and blind.

We are created
with the capacity to love
and be loved in return.
But, rather than find the lost causes
people would watch them burn.
Cast them out,
shame them,
isolate them
because it's what they
"deserve".

It's so easy to hate
when your heart is hurting.

It's difficult to love
those who are difficult to love
but we should anyway.
Not because it's simple
but because it's right.
Who are we to decide
what way our souls collide?

I could hold the universe
in the palm of my hand,
but if I have not love
I am nothing.

This is a love poem
because love is everything.

Stormy Weather

The rain plummets diagonally this time.
Touching everything and leaving its mark.
Dark clouds,
                    Wind howling,
                                        Thunder rolling.

How can we be peaceful
when the rain is beating down?
When the gales are high
and the lightning flashes
and your jacket
just doesn't quite
keep you dry?
And when the cold hits
and your hair starts to drip
and your cries are useless
because nobody can
hear you anyway
and the world is full
of anger
and hurt
and revenge
and pointless violence
and people are killed
for no apparent reason
and there are grudges
and guns
and wars
and politics
and

How can we be peaceful
when everything else is not?

When the thunder grips your heart
and you can't see
thanks to the rain that
came from nowhere
and the boat almost capsizes
and you cry out in terror
"Save us, Lord!"

What does He do?

Stands,
raises His arms,
breathes.

You of little faith,
why did you doubt?

Beauty is in the eye of the beholder,
peace is in the eye of the storm.

When you stand in the rain
but it doesn't get you wet
because you don't let it
and you stop for a second
and listen to the
perfect, uneven tapping
of the rain droplets
as they fall from the overhang
onto the window ledge
and you notice
the washing on the line;
left out too long and
too far gone to save now.
The deep breaths you take
as you allow the petrichor
to fill your lungs.

Do not let your heart be troubled,
do not be afraid.

Close your eyes,

inhale,

exhale,

and listen to the rain
dance to the
rhythm of your
tired soul.

Faithful

You met me in that place tonight
With arms stretched open wide.
You took me in, and cleaned me up,
And held me as I cried.
I know that you are faithful
As you've been here all along.
You carried me when I could not walk
'Cause in my weakness you are strong.
My soul is as a barren land
And death is all I know,
But you tended to this garden
And, now, your goodness there will grow.
And though I am clothed in shadow,
And darkness enters in,
Still, I believe your grace will triumph
And your light will always win.

The light
shines in the
darkness
and the
darkness
has not
overcome it

JOHN 1:5

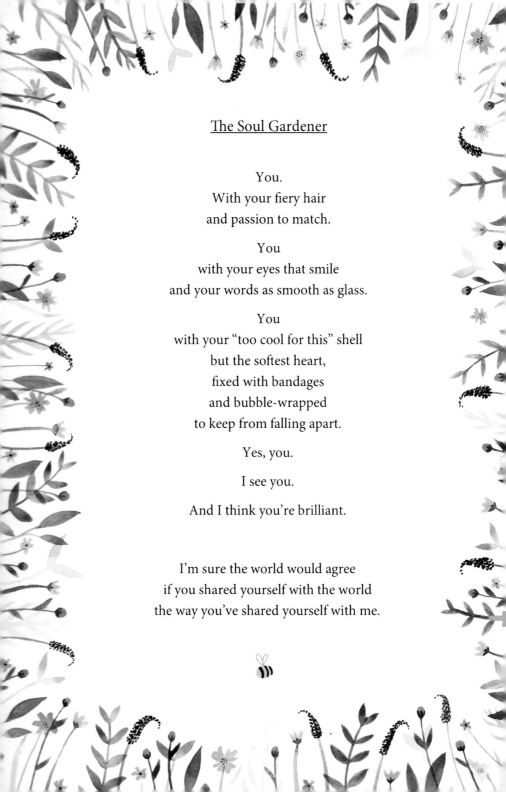

The Soul Gardener

You.
With your fiery hair
and passion to match.

You
with your eyes that smile
and your words as smooth as glass.

You
with your "too cool for this" shell
but the softest heart,
fixed with bandages
and bubble-wrapped
to keep from falling apart.

Yes, you.

I see you.

And I think you're brilliant.

I'm sure the world would agree
if you shared yourself with the world
the way you've shared yourself with me.

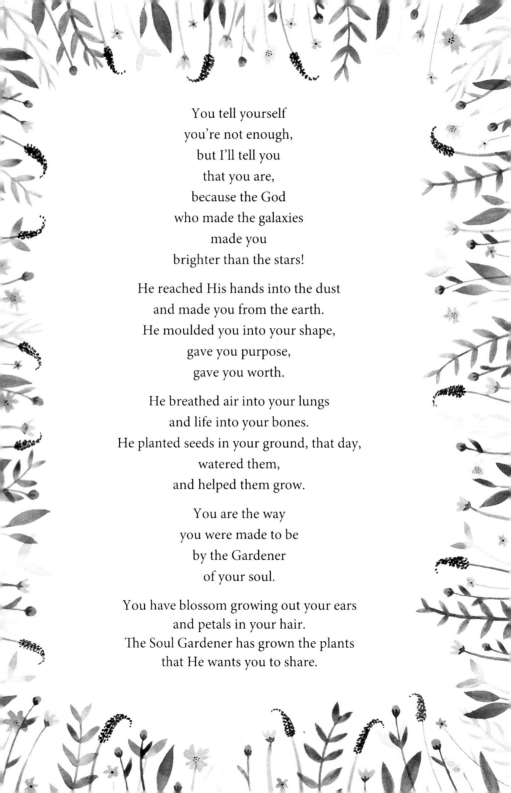

You tell yourself
you're not enough,
but I'll tell you
that you are,
because the God
who made the galaxies
made you
brighter than the stars!

He reached His hands into the dust
and made you from the earth.
He moulded you into your shape,
gave you purpose,
gave you worth.

He breathed air into your lungs
and life into your bones.
He planted seeds in your ground, that day,
watered them,
and helped them grow.

You are the way
you were made to be
by the Gardener
of your soul.

You have blossom growing out your ears
and petals in your hair.
The Soul Gardener has grown the plants
that He wants you to share.

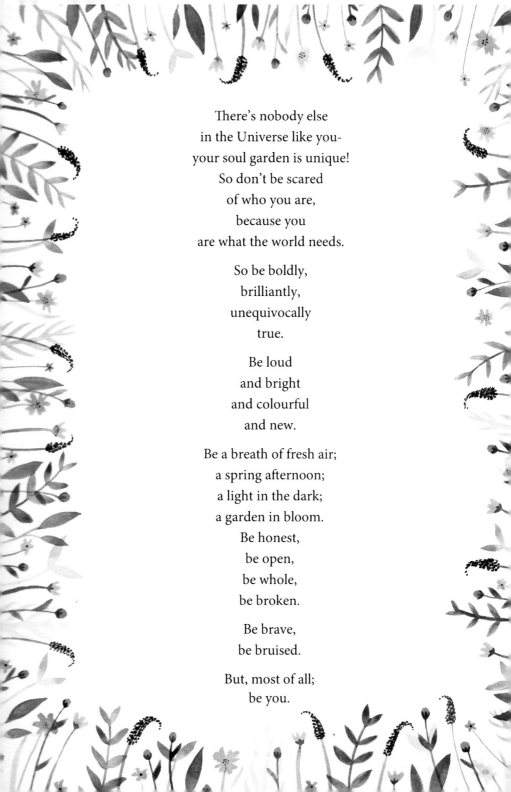

There's nobody else
in the Universe like you-
your soul garden is unique!
So don't be scared
of who you are,
because you
are what the world needs.

So be boldly,
brilliantly,
unequivocally
true.

Be loud
and bright
and colourful
and new.

Be a breath of fresh air;
a spring afternoon;
a light in the dark;
a garden in bloom.
Be honest,
be open,
be whole,
be broken.

Be brave,
be bruised.

But, most of all;
be you.

and my
Father
is the
gardener

JOHN 15:1

About the Illustrator

Graceful Designs is a small business run on-the-side of real life by the fantastic Grace Scott. She started the venture in January 2018 and produces beautiful watercolour prints, custom wedding stationary, bespoke personal orders, and much more.

You can find more of Graceful Designs on:

Facebook . . . . @graceful.designs5
Instagram . . . . @gracefuldesignsuk
Etsy . . . . GracefulDesignsUK

Or send an e-mail via graceful.designs5@gmail.com

Huge amounts of love to Grace for getting on board with this crazy /wonderful idea, and providing us with a set of utterly gorgeous illustrations. They are so perfect for this book, and I could not have done this without you. Thankyou.

About the Author

Beth is a 22-year-old amateur poet and professional procrastinator from Hull, UK. Her poetry journey began in 2017, and she decided to release this collection in the hopes that it will bring some sunshine to those who encounter it.
Her poetry is inspired by her surroundings, her experiences, and her faith.

You can find more of Beth's poetry on:

Instagram . . . . @soulgardenpoems
Her website . . . . soulgarden.blog

Any questions/comments/enquiries, please get in touch with Beth by e-mailing bethacpoetry@gmail.com

Thankyou to everyone who has supported and encouraged me on this journey. You are invaluable.